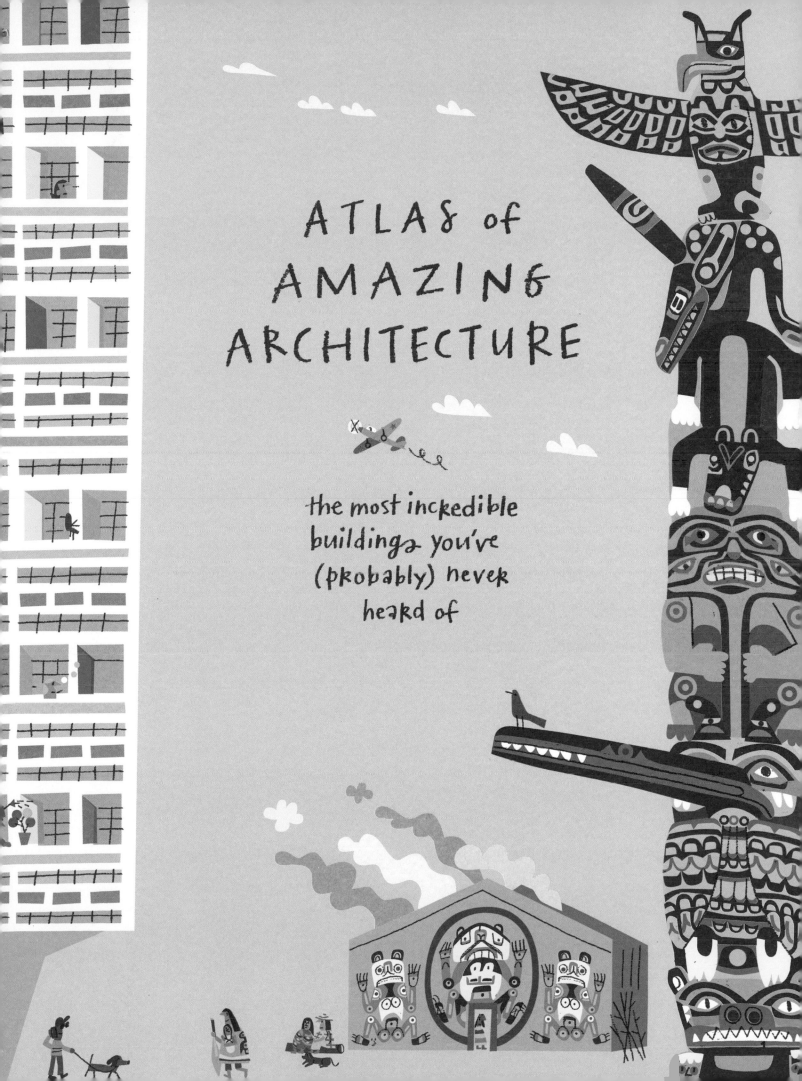

ATLAS of AMAZING ARCHITECTURE

the most inckedible
buildings you've
(pkobably) nevek
heakd of

CONTENTS

INTRODUCTION

For thousands of years humans have been stacking stones, laying bricks or lashing wood together to create structures in which to live, work and worship.

ARCHITECTURE SHOULD SPEAK OF ITS TIME
AND PLACE BUT YEARN FOR TIMELESSNESS.
– FRANK GEHRY

The buildings they make have stories; about the history and culture that brought them into being, the landscape and environment in which they were constructed, or about the person who designed or built them.

Sometimes these stories are complex, because architecture itself is complex. To build a building, you need to understand the physics of structures, so that it doesn't fall down. You need to know what materials and technologies are available to you. You need to understand how people might want to use a space, and you need money. Often quite a lot of money. Last but not least, it helps to have a vision – of how the space will look inside and out, and how you can put your own personal stamp on it.

The buildings in this book have amazing stories. We tried to steer clear of the buildings that everyone knows (the Great Pyramids or the Eiffel Tower, for example), instead choosing buildings around the world and throughout history that are less well known, but have forged new ground in the way they look or the way they were designed. For example, you'll find the story of a king who carved great churches out of rock, because he believed he was destined to build a new Jerusalem in the mountains of Ethiopia. Or a mosque in Iran that has been added to and embellished over the course of 2,000 years. You'll even find the story of a building that was never made, but which captured the spirit (and also the follies) of the Russian Revolution. A lot of the buildings have an expressive, sculptural quality to them, because often a strange looking building has a strange sounding story behind it.

This is by no means a comprehensive introduction to architecture – it's just a starting point for thinking and talking about different types of buildings. Take the room you're sitting in right now, for example. How does it make you feel? Is there a window? What kind of window is it? What's the view? Is the building similar to other buildings around it? What makes it unique? Once you start really looking at the buildings around you, you'll see their stories emerge, because the stories of buildings and the stories of people are inextricably intertwined.

– Peter Allen and Ziggy Hanaor

NEOLITHIC MONUMENTS

WHEN: 4000–2000 BCE
WHERE: NORTHERN EUROPE

**Newgrange Burial Mound
Ireland, 3200 BCE**

The Neolithic period lasted from around 7000 BCE to 1700 BCE. There was no written history, so very little is known about it. In Europe, a handful of mysterious monuments are all that remain. They are mostly burial chambers, made from mounds of earth, and standing stones, which were probably part of religious rituals.

A vast burial mound surrounded by a wall of engraved stones. On the winter solstice, the rising sun floods the inner burial chamber with light.

**The Carnac Stones
France, 3300 BCE**

A collection of over 3,000 standing stones, some as tall as four metres, arranged in 11 rows, a kilometre long, with stone circles at either end.

Avebury, England, 3000–2400 BCE

A henge (meaning a bank and a ditch) that contains three large stone circles. It was probably a regional hub for religious ceremonies, trading and feasting.

Skara Brae
Scotland, 3000 BCE

In the remote Orkney Islands lies Europe's most complete Neolithic village, made up of eight stone houses built into the ground for insulation. They contain stone furniture and even toilets.

ZIGGURAT OF UR

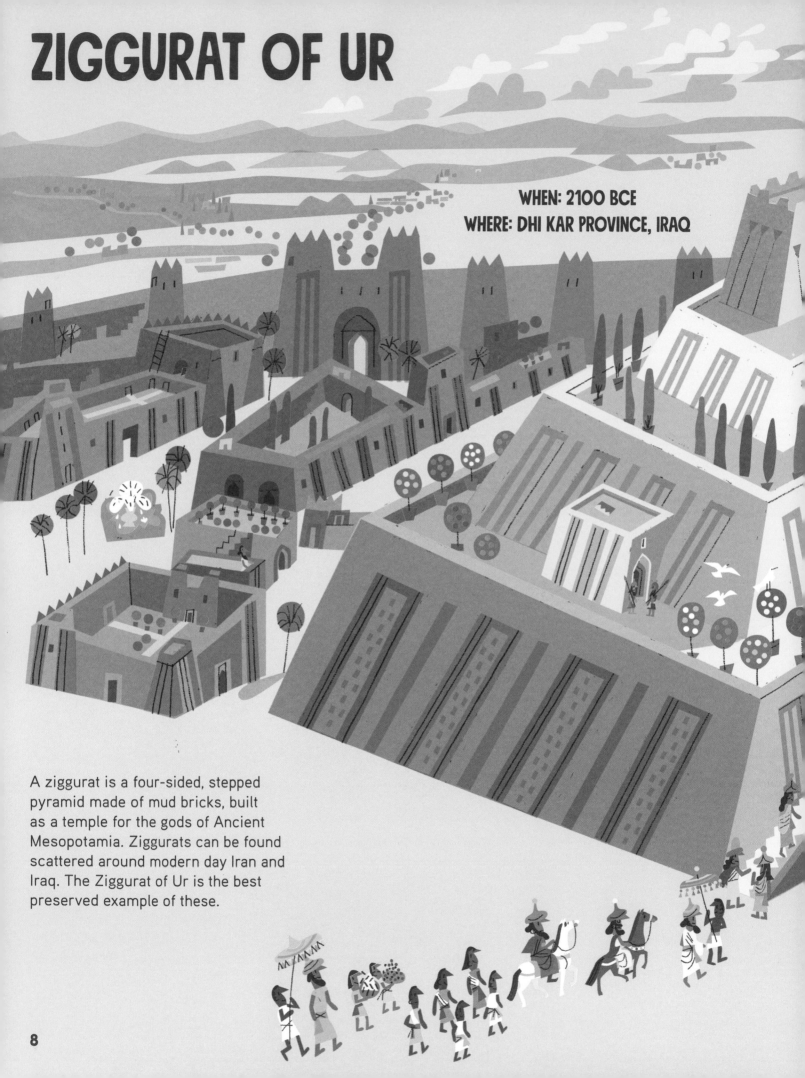

WHEN: 2100 BCE
WHERE: DHI KAR PROVINCE, IRAQ

A ziggurat is a four-sided, stepped pyramid made of mud bricks, built as a temple for the gods of Ancient Mesopotamia. Ziggurats can be found scattered around modern day Iran and Iraq. The Ziggurat of Ur is the best preserved example of these.

Built by King Ur-Nammu in honour of the moon-god, Nanna, the ziggurat was part of a temple complex at the heart of the great city of Ur. At 64 m long and 30 m high, the ziggurat would have been visible for miles around, a symbol of the city's wealth.

Only the foundations of the structure survive, but originally, Nanna's temple would have perched at the top of the structure, decorated with blue glazed bricks. The gods were thought to live in their temples and so Nanna's temple would have included a bedroom where he could sleep, and a kitchen where mortal servants could prepare his food.

The temple fell to ruin, but was restored in the 6th century BCE. It was then abandoned once more and forgotten until its remains were excavated in the 1920s. It was restored once more in the 1980s.

MEROE PYRAMIDS

In the desert of Sudan, on the east bank of the Nile, lies a collection of over 200 ancient pyramids; the remains of the city of Meroe, capital of the great kingdom of Kush.

These pyramids, built of granite and sandstone, are called Nubian pyramids.

Built 1,000 years after their Egyptian cousins, They have a narrower base and steeper slopes. They measure anywhere between six and 30 metres high, and often have a temple structure at their base.

When the pyramids were discovered in the 1830s, they were looted by tomb raiders, who destroyed the top parts of many of the pyramids in their attempts to reach the treasures within.

They served as tombs for kings, queens and nobles, who were mummified and buried with jewels and other earthly belongings. These belongings came from all across the vast Kush empire, which stretched from the Mediterranean deep into the heart of Africa.

SHANXI HANGING MONASTERY

WHEN: 491 CE
WHERE: SHANXI PROVINCE, CHINA

This gravity-defying temple is built into the cliff of Cuiping Peak, 76 m off the ground. It is secured in place with oak crossbeams that are chiselled into the rockface behind it.

According to legend, the temple was constructed by one man, a monk named Liaoran, of the Northern Wei dynasty, who had a vision of a place where monks could meditate without any distraction from the surrounding land.

Interestingly, the temple is dedicated not to one religion, but three – Confucianism, Taoism and Buddhism, with religious carvings and statues from all of them dotted throughout the temple. This is because the monastery once served as an important resting station for pilgrims passing through the area, and all were welcomed, regardless of religion.

The overhanging lip of the cliff protects the monastery from rain, snow and floods, and, apart from a few renovations and additions, most of the original structure is preserved.

HAGIA SOFIA

WHEN: 537 CE
WHERE: ISTANBUL (FORMERLY CONSTANTINOPLE), TURKEY

The Hagia Sophia (meaning 'Holy Wisdom' in Greek) was a great church in the heart of Constantinople, the capital of the Byzantine Empire. It was built by the Roman Emperor Justinian I as proof of his power. Completed in just six years, the church was the largest building in the world for many hundreds of years.

It features a great domed roof of about 33 m in diameter. A dome this size without any steel enforcements is still considered a marvel of engineering.

Originally, the building was clad in shimmering white marble. Inside, it was decorated with golden mosaics and treasures from the far reaches of the Byzantine Empire.

The building served as a church until 1453, when the Ottoman Empire converted it into a mosque, adding four minarets and destroying many of the original features.

The Hagia Sophia influenced eastern architecture for years to come. Today it serves as a museum.

15

ANJI BRIDGE

WHEN: 595–605 CE
WHERE: HEBEI PROVINCE, CHINA

The Anji Bridge (meaning 'Safe Crossing Bridge'), was built during the reign of the powerful Sui dynasty. It crosses the Xiao River, connecting important trade routes across China.

The bridge was designed by a craftsman called Li Chun. Up until that point, bridges were mostly built in a single semi-circular arch. Chun's design was an engineering breakthrough, as the main arch is supported by two smaller arches on either side.

This clever design meant that the arch could be much less steep, making the bridge easier to cross. It also allowed for a lighter construction, using 40 percent fewer materials.

The central arch is made of 28 thin, curved limestone slabs joined with iron rivets. This allows the bridge to shift, meaning that it won't collapse, even if part of the arch breaks.

In times of flood, the water is diverted through the smaller arches, putting less pressure on each individual arch.

Still standing 1,400 years later, it has survived eight wars, ten floods, and several earthquakes. It is the oldest stone bridge of its kind in the world.

HORYU-JI TEMPLES

WHEN: 607 CE
WHERE: KANSAI REGION, JAPAN

The temple complex of Horyu-ji contains 26 wooden buildings including a five-storey pagoda, which is the oldest wooden structure in the world.

The complex was commissioned by Prince Shotuko, who brought the Buddhist religion from China over to Japan. The buildings were constructed using traditional Chinese techniques, which later became common in the region.

Horyu-ji was dedicated to Yakushi Nyorai, the Buddha of healing. It is said that a fragment of the bones of the Buddha is enshrined at the base of the pagoda.

The ornate buildings are typical of the era. Heavy tiled roofs are supported by wooden brackets with beautiful dragon carvings.

The buildings are constructed on double terrace platforms. Many of them feature columns which curve and taper slightly, so that they seem perfectly straight when viewed from a distance.

JAMEH MOSQUE OF ISFAHAN

WHEN: 771–1997 CE
WHERE: ISFAHAN, IRAN

Built over the course of 12 centuries, this vast mosque shows us how Islamic architecture developed through the ages.

It was built in the 11th century by the Seljuk Turks on the site of an earlier mosque, which had burned down. The Seljuks established Isfahan as their capital and built the central mosque in a new, four-iwan style. An *iwan* is a vaulted room that opens on one side to a courtyard. The gates of the four iwans are positioned face to face to create a huge central courtyard.

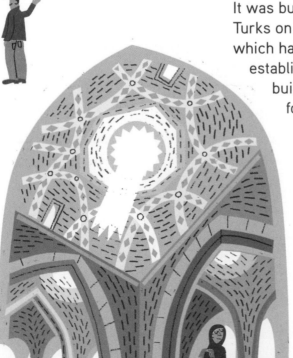

Originally, all the four gates would have been open, making the courtyard a pedestrian hub at the heart of the city; a place for business and community relations as well as a place for worship.

After the Seljuk Empire, the mosque was embellished and added to by the various rulers of Persia, so that it grew to cover an area of over 20,000 m². Its internal decorations reflect changing Islamic styles through the ages.

Two spectacular 11th century domes are architectural highlights. They were built using a 'double-shell ribbed' structure in order to create perfect proportion and balance. This required brand new engineering skills that were later used throughout the Islamic world.

CHAND BAORI

WHEN: 800 CE
WHERE: RAJASTHAN, INDIA

A 'baori' is a type of well surrounded by steps that is unique to India. It provides access to bathing and drinking water for communities in dry regions like Rajasthan.

Chand Baori is the biggest and most impressive of the Indian step-wells. Built by King Chandra of the Nikumbha dynasty, 3,500 narrow steps are arranged in perfect symmetry around three sides of a large well. The fourth side features an intricately carved stone pavilion with elegant galleries and balconies, which was added to over many centuries.

The play of light and shadow on the steps changes throughout the day, turning it into a visual maze.

The steps descend 20 m into the ground, with the air at the bottom of the well around six degrees cooler than at the surface. The well served not just as a place to drink and bathe but also to meditate, pray and socialise during the heat of the day. Royals would shelter in the pavilion, whilst the commoners would gather on the lower steps.

23

CHARTRES CATHEDRAL

WHEN: 1194–1220
WHERE: CHARTRES, FRANCE

This cathedral in North West France is an example of French Gothic architecture. This style of architecture was all about height – creating towering spires that would be visible for miles around, showing the world how pious and wealthy a town was.

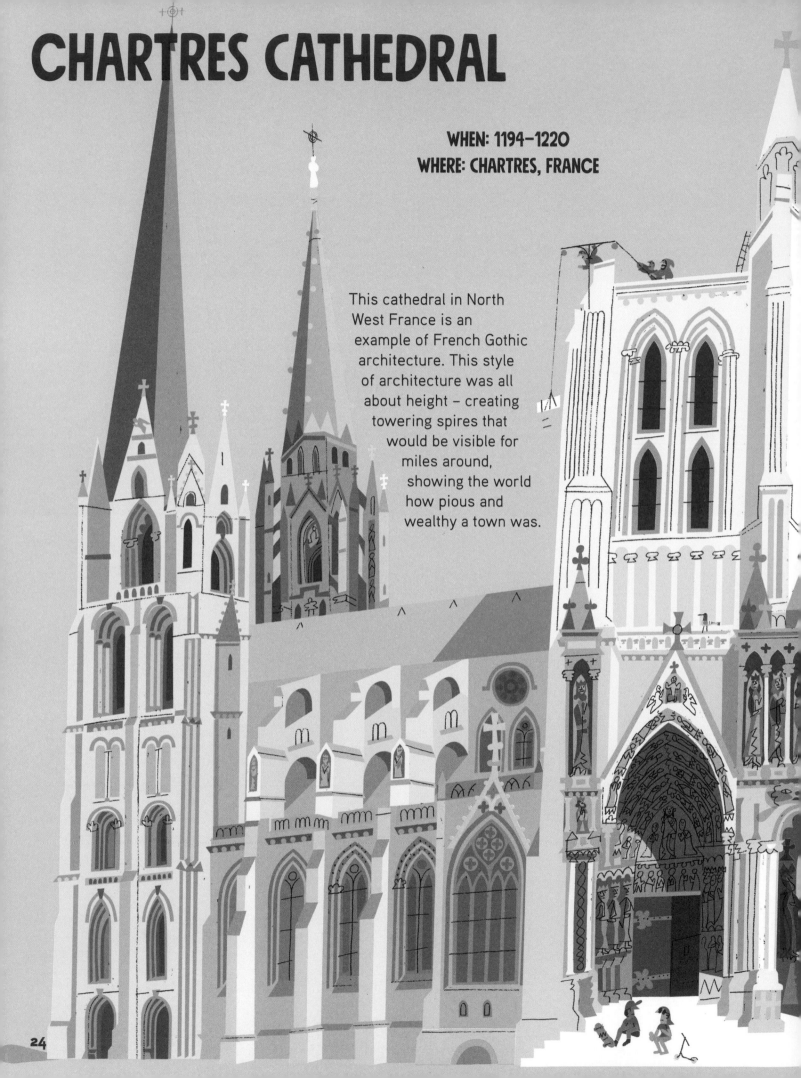

In order to achieve this height, Chartres Cathedral makes use of flying buttresses. These are arches that reach from high up an outside wall to a pier some distance away. They carry the weight of the tall, slender building, allowing the walls to be taken up by 176 elaborate stained-glass windows that fill the space with dramatic light.

Throughout the cathedral there are hundreds of sculptures of biblical figures in the dramatic poses favoured by the Gothic style.

The cathedral features many classic qualities of Gothic architecture including pointed arches and ornate sculptural decorations. It is said to contain a holy relic; a fragment of a tunic worn by the Virgin Mary. This made it a popular destination for Christian pilgrims through the ages and until today.

BORGUND STAVE CHURCH

WHEN: CA. 1200
WHERE: BORGUND, NORWAY

Stave churches are small churches with walls made of vertical wooden boards, or staves. They were common in medieval times in rural communities around Scandinavia, where wood was plentiful. Most stave churches were destroyed and replaced with stone churches in the 19th century, but 28 still stand in Norway.

The church in the small town of Borgund is one of the best preserved examples. It has tiered overhanging roofs, topped by a turret. The tiered roofs protect the building from the rain and snow.

On the gables, there are four carved dragon heads, like those that can be seen on Norse ships. The main portal of the church features intricate carvings of flowers, fighting snakes and flying dragons.

The simple space inside probably once featured other decorative carvings, which have since been lost or destroyed. On the west wall of the church, ancient graffiti runes are etched into the wall, one of which reads, 'Thor wrote these runes on the evening of the St Olav's Mass.'

CHURCH OF ST GEORGE

WHEN: CA. 1200
WHERE: LALIBELA, ETHIOPIA

The Church of St George is an example of monolithic architecture; buildings that are carved or cast from a single piece of material, in this case, volcanic rock.

It was built by King Lalibela, who, according to legend, was instructed by God to create a new Jerusalem in the mountains of central Ethiopia.

A group of 11 monolithic churches were carved out of the rock with a trench running through the middle, symbolising the River Jordan. One side of the 'river' represents earthly Jerusalem and the other, heavenly Jerusalem.

The Church of St George is the most elaborate of the churches. It is a cross-shaped building carved downwards into the mountain, with windows, doors and delicate engravings chiselled into the stone.

Inside, there is a simple shrine to St George and a replica of the Ark of the Covenant.

The church can only be entered by way of a hidden canyon, so that from above it looks like it's completely inaccessible.

Lalibela is one of Ethiopia's holiest places, and a destination for Christian pilgrims.

DOGE'S PALACE

WHEN: 1340–1424
WHERE: VENICE, ITALY

The Palazzo Ducale, or Doge's Palace, is one of Venice's most striking buildings. The palace served as the residence for the chosen ruler of Venice, the Doge.

It was also the centre of government for the powerful and wealthy Venetian Republic.

There is a rhythm to the design of the building. Large Gothic pointed arches are topped by smaller pointed arches which give way to elaborate patterns of pink and white stone. Ornamental points along the top accentuate the patterns below.

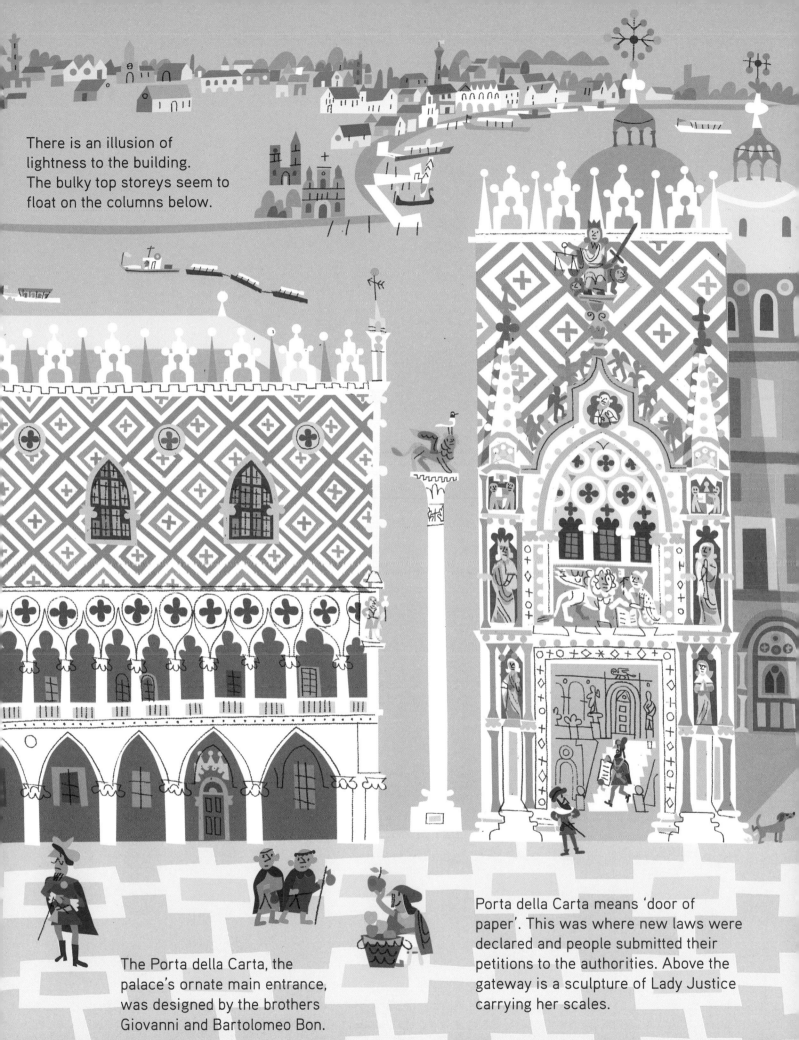

There is an illusion of lightness to the building. The bulky top storeys seem to float on the columns below.

The Porta della Carta, the palace's ornate main entrance, was designed by the brothers Giovanni and Bartolomeo Bon.

Porta della Carta means 'door of paper'. This was where new laws were declared and people submitted their petitions to the authorities. Above the gateway is a sculpture of Lady Justice carrying her scales.

DJINGUEREBER MOSQUE

WHEN: 1327
WHERE: TIMBUKTU, MALI

Djinguereber is a mosque and a madrassa, forming part of the University of Timbuktu. It is made almost entirely of mud. The mosque was commissioned by Emperor Moussa I, possibly the wealthiest man that ever lived.

The emperor allegedly paid 200 kg of gold to a Spanish-Egyptian poet, Abu Es Haq es Saheli, to design the mosque. The elegant, organic building features two pyramid shaped minarets, three inner courts and space for 2,000 congregants. It is unlikely that Saheli designed it all himself without help from an architect.

The mosque is made of a material called banco, a mixture of fermented mud and grain husks, which is formed into bricks. It has to be dug out of the ground, like peat.

When the mosque was built, Timbuktu was a wealthy oasis town, but today the city is poor and suffers from desertification – the expansion of the Sahara Desert as a result of climate change.

Banco, therefore, is increasingly hard to source. Also, the resulting droughts and flash floods damage the delicate mud construction, and the mosque needs constant maintenance. Sometimes there are maintenance festivals, when everyone has fun getting very muddy!

AYUTTHAYA

The city of Ayutthaya was once the capital of the powerful Siamese kingdom. Located on an island surrounded by three rivers at the halfway point between India and China, it became a vital connecting point to the spoils of the east. People came from as far and wide as China, Japan, Portugal, Persia and England.

Although Ayutthaya was burned to the ground by the Burmese army in 1767, its remains reflect the city's past magnificence. The buildings mostly fall into two categories: *chedi*, which have mound-like bases and elegant, pointed spires, and *prang*, which are taller, corn-cob-like structures that represent nearby Mount Meru.

By the early 18th century, its population had reached 1,000,000 people – making it one of the largest and most cosmopolitan cities in the world. It was known as the 'Venice of the East' due to its many canals.

34

The monastery Wat Pra Si Sanphet is a chedi, with three dramatically pointed pagodas. Built in 1350, it once served as the royal chapel, and featured a statue of the Buddha coated in 170 kg of gold.

Wat Mahathat is a prang structure with intricate carvings. It contains holy Buddhist relics.

LITTLE MORETON HALL

WHEN: 1504–1610
WHERE: CHESHIRE, UNITED KINGDOM

Little Moreton Hall is an example of truly eccentric British architecture. The Moreton family became rich by buying up land after the Black Death and built a house to show off their new prosperity. Although it was already the height of the Renaissance in England, they chose to build it in a medieval 'half-timbered' style, in which the wooden frame of the house is made visible.

The façade of the house is very decorative, with the timbers forming chevron and lozenge patterns. This style was common in Germany, but less so in Britain.

The shape of the building is also very odd. It is asymmetrical, with the third floor sticking out over the bottom two floors and a long gallery running the length of it. It has been described by some as a 'stranded Noah's Ark'.

Inside, there are almost no corridors. Rooms lead off each other and it's hard to tell what they would have been used for. The building is surrounded by a moat that serves no purpose at all.

Little Moreton Hall is thought to be haunted; a grey lady is said to walk up and down the long gallery, and in the chapel, a ghostly child has been heard sobbing.

TRADITIONAL
JAPANESE ARCHITECTURE

Traditional Japanese buildings are almost always made of wood, never of stone. They are lifted slightly off the ground and often feature large roofs that curve out beyond the walls, creating a shady space within. Inside, there is usually a single big space with sliding screens instead of walls that can break up the room as required. The environment of the building is carefully considered, and the buildings are designed to fit into their natural surrounds.

Shinto Shrine

A Shinto shrine is used for the safekeeping of sacred objects (*kami*). They usually have elaborate roofs, and a veranda that wraps around the building. The *kami* is kept in a sanctuary called a *honden*. Older temples will sometimes have a Buddhist temple inside or next to the shrine.

Katsura Imperial Villa, 1645

This complex of royal residences, shrines and tea houses is a classic example of traditional architecture. The buildings are set into carefully designed gardens, with screen walls that connect the buildings to the outside world. Raised floors are covered in grids of rush mats called *tatami*.

Japanese Tea Houses

The tea ceremonies of Japan are spiritual rituals that draw from Zen Buddhism. They are about patience, humility and acceptance. They are hosted in simple, modest buildings set into nature and designed to promote a sense of peace and tranquillity.

KIZHI POGOST

On an island in the centre of Lake Onega, in northern Russia's remote Karelia region, stand three wooden structures, two churches and a belfry, that are examples of the incredible carpentry traditions that were once commonplace in the area. No nails were used in their construction except in the domes and the roof shingles.

48

Legend has it that the lead builder, Master Nestor, used a single axe for the whole construction. When he finished, he threw it into the lake with the words: 'There was not and will not be another one to match it.'

The most impressive of the buildings is the Church of Transfiguration. Built on the site of an older church, it features 22 domes of different sizes and shapes.

The church is one of the oldest wooden structures in Europe. Inside there is an elaborate iconostasis – a wooden screen covered with carved religious icons.

CASBAH OF ALGIERS

WHEN: 17TH–18TH CENTURIES
WHERE: ALGIERS, ALGERIA

The Casbah is the walled old quarter of the city of Algiers; a slope of white buildings leading down to the Mediterranean Sea. The city was built in the 10th century but was destroyed in an earthquake. Most of what stands today was built during the rule of the Ottoman Empire. As well as houses, the Casbah contains many mosques and palaces.

The Casbah was once home to wealthy caliphs (Muslim rulers) as well as pirates. In the 1950s and '60s, its winding streets offered shelter to rebels fighting for independence from the French colonial rule.

The Dar Mustapha Pacha is a Moorish Palace within the Casbah. Built around a grand courtyard, it features arched galleries, wooden-beamed ceilings and beautiful tile-work. Built in 1798, it is one of the few major buildings that was not damaged during the French occupation.

HWAESEONG FORTRESS

WHEN: 1794–1796
WHERE: SUWON, SOUTH KOREA

Hwaeseong is a stone and brick fortress that surrounds the city of Suwon. It was built by King Jeongjo in response to the wars with Japan that were happening at the time. Rather than building a mountain fortress to escape to, the king decided to fortify the walls of the city itself.

The walls surround an area of around 1.3 km². They incorporate arrow launcher towers, secret gates, observation towers, bunkers and a vast royal palace. They also contain a tomb for King Jeongjo's father, who was brutally executed by his own father by being locked alive inside a rice chest.

King Jeongjo worked with an architect called Jeong Yakyong, who was the leader of the Practical Learning Movement. This movement encouraged the use of science and industry, and brought together the latest techniques in design and construction from both Europe and Asia.

Complex pulley systems were used to construct the fortress. These cutting edge building methods were used throughout Korea for many years to come.

BRIGHTON PAVILION

WHEN: 1787–1823
WHERE: BRIGHTON, UNITED KINGDOM

Brighton's Royal Pavilion, with its fanciful domes, minarets and spires, is a bizarre sight in the middle of a British seaside town. It was originally designed as a 'marine pavilion' for King George III (known as the 'mad king'), who wanted a beach retreat in the up-and-coming city of Brighton.

When his son came to the throne, the young prince regent went even further, commissioning the architect John Nash to transform the building into a pleasure palace. Inspired by the treasures coming back from colonial India and China, Nash designed a multi-domed building that has more in common with the Taj Mahal than with the architecture that surrounds it.

Inside, the Chinese and Indian influences continue with exotic murals and luxuriant decoration from all corners of the British Empire. The chandelier in the Banqueting Room weighs over one ton. The walls of the Music Room are covered in gold silk and its domed ceiling is studded with hundreds of gilded cockleshells.

Queen Victoria disapproved of the building and of the indulgences of her forbearers, and in 1850 sold it to the city of Brighton for £50,000.

NEUSCHWANSTEIN CASTLE

Neuschwanstein (New Swan Stone) Castle was designed and built by Ludwig II, an embattled Bavarian king, on the site of a ruined castle in the foothills of the Alps.

Ludwig was nostalgic for simpler times, and he merged various architectural styles to create an idealised intepretation of a medieval knight's castle.

A keen opera enthusiast, Ludwig built the castle in honour of his close friend, the composer Richard Wagner.

He spared no expense. Rooms were finished with marble, murals and mosaics. A fairytale grotto included a manmade canal complete with ornate swan-boats. Despite its medieval style, Ludwig insisted on using the latest 19th century technologies such as steel beams, telephone lines, flushing toilets and central heating.

As costs spiralled out of control, Ludwig's government rebelled and Ludwig died in mysterious circumstances in 1886, having slept a total of 11 nights at the castle. Only a handful of rooms were completed. The rest of the building was finished in simpler form after his death.

If the castle looks familiar that's probably because it was the inspiration behind Disney's famous Sleeping Beauty Castle. Ludwig's fantasy lives on!

CHIEF WAKA'S HOUSE

WHEN: CA. 1890
WHERE: ALERT BAY, BRITISH COLUMBIA, CANADA

When the Europeans reached Canada in the late 18th century, they brought with them smallpox and influenza, which wiped out swathes of the indigenous populations of the Pacific Northwest. These diseases particularly affected older people, who, as respected elders, were the leaders of communities. Within 50 years, many cultures, traditions and even languages had been lost.

Chief Waka, of the Kwakwa'ka'wakw nation, built a house that was a statement of pride in a heritage that was already on the verge of extinction. It was constructed in a plank-house style that had been used by indigenous peoples for almost 3,000 years, with overlapping cedar planks protecting it from the wind and snow.

Outside the front stood a magnificent totem pole with emblems of the chief's family history. At the top of the pole is Thunderbird, Lord of the Upper World, then Killer Whale, Lord of the Sea, then Wolf, Wise One (a human), Cannibal Bird and Bear. At the base is Raven, whose great beak opened to become a ceremonial entrance to the house.

CASA BATLLO

WHEN: 1904–1906
WHERE: BARCELONA, SPAIN

The architect Antoni Gaudi was given free rein to refurbish a home in the centre of Barcelona for the wealthy Batllo family.

Gaudi had a very unique architectural style. Designing his buildings using models, rather than drawing them out, Gaudi paid attention to every detail, thinking about how ceramics, stained glass, ironwork and other crafts might be incorporated into the designs.

Casa Batllo is also known as Casa dels Ossos, or House of Bones, because it looks a bit like a giant dragon skeleton. It has gaping oval windows, bony balconies and very few straight lines. The broken tiles that cover its façade ripple like scales.

The roof is arched and spiny, with colourful mosaic tiles. At one end, there is a turret and a cross, representing the sword that St George plunged into the back of the dragon.

At the other end, a small triangular window looks like the eye of the dragon.

Gaudi was a devout Catholic, and religious motifs such as the story of St George often appear in his buildings.

TATLIN'S TOWER

Vladimir Tatlin's fantastical iron and glass tower is probably the most famous building never built. It was designed in the early days of Soviet Russia as part of a programme to replace the monuments of the old regime with new ones that would reflect the ideas of the Russian Revolution.

Tatlin, an architect and painter, envisaged a giant, red iron structure, twice the size of the Eiffel Tower, which would straddle the river Neva, spiralling out of the ground at a dynamic 60° angle.

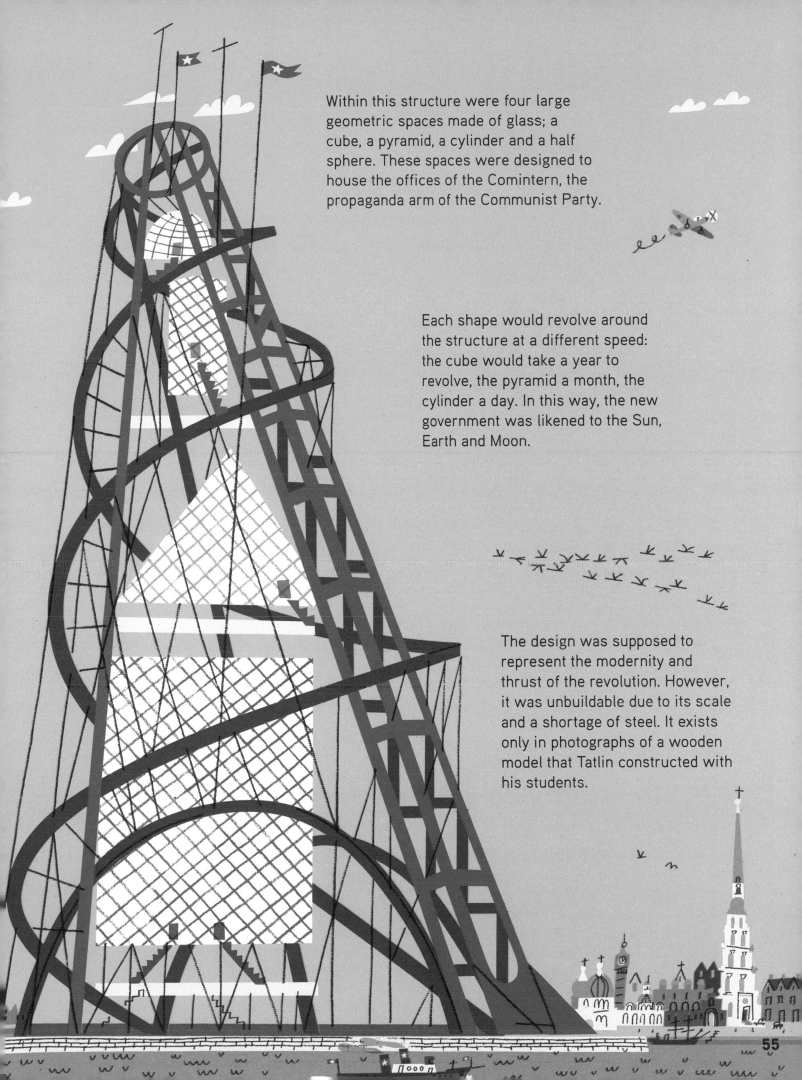

Within this structure were four large geometric spaces made of glass; a cube, a pyramid, a cylinder and a half sphere. These spaces were designed to house the offices of the Comintern, the propaganda arm of the Communist Party.

Each shape would revolve around the structure at a different speed: the cube would take a year to revolve, the pyramid a month, the cylinder a day. In this way, the new government was likened to the Sun, Earth and Moon.

The design was supposed to represent the modernity and thrust of the revolution. However, it was unbuildable due to its scale and a shortage of steel. It exists only in photographs of a wooden model that Tatlin constructed with his students.

DAR AL-HAJAR PALACE

WHEN: 1920
WHERE: WADI DA'AR, YEMEN

This fantastical palace was built on top of an existing 18th century building. Commissioned by the spiritual leader, Imam Yahya Muhammad Hamiddin, it looks like an magnificent gingerbread house.

Dar al-Hajar was intended as a summer palace, a retreat from the hustle and bustle of the city.

The palace is made of the same stone as the cliff it is perched upon, and it's hard to tell where the rock ends and the palace begins. Inside, the palace is a labyrinth of corridors, staircases and rooms. Now serving as a museum, it is a much-loved icon of Yemenite architecture.

RIETVELD SCHRÖDER HOUSE

WHEN: 1924

WHERE: UTRECHT, THE NETHERLANDS

Truus Schröder, a young widow, wanted a house that would offer her and her three children a modern, flexible way of living. She commissioned a young furniture designer, Gerrit Rietveld, to help her realise this ambition. At the time, he had never designed a building before.

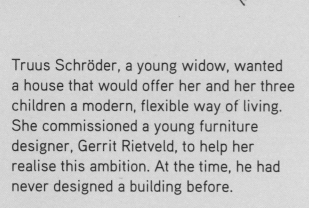

Rietveld was a member of an artistic movement called De Stijl, which sought to reduce forms to their bare essentials.

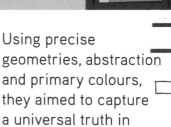

Using precise geometries, abstraction and primary colours, they aimed to capture a universal truth in their designs.

The main space of the house was designed without walls but with a system of sliding and revolving panels that could divide the space up into private rooms.

Highlights of primary colours emphasise the geometric elements of the design.

The outside of the house is made up of planes and lines that seem to glide past each other, occasionally meeting to form a balcony.

The big windows allowed the view of the forest outside to become part of the living space. Unfortunately, a busy road later took the place of the forest.

Schröder and Rietveld collaborated on a number of other buildings, but Schröder never received credit for these projects.

WORLD'S FAIRS

After the Industrial Revolution, progress in technology and science came along in leaps and bounds. Western countries began to host international exhibitions in which they could showcase their achievements. These fairs lasted months on end, and were often marked with structures that captured the latest radical ideas and building technologies.

**Crystal Palace
London, UK, 1851**

The first officially recognised World's Fair was the 'Great Exhibition of the Works of Industry of All Nations' in London. Sheet glass was a new invention, and architect Joseph Paxton used it to great effect in a vast palace of cast iron and glass. It was later relocated and burned down in 1936.

**Mies Van Der Rohe Pavilion
Barcelona, Spain, 1929**

After the first world war, Germany wanted to project a peace-loving image to the world. Architect Mies Van Der Rohe designed a sleek, minimalist German pavilion for the Barcelona World's Fair with a low flat roof that seemed to float. He used luxurious materials that reflected a new internationalism.

Atomium
Brussels, Belgium, 1958

The atomic age of the 1950s was captured in this World Expo pavilion that was designed to look like nine atoms in the shape of an iron crystal. Each 'atom' sphere contains an exhibition hall, which is connected to the next by tubes containing escalators.

Space Needle
Seattle, USA, 1962

This iconic tower reflects the spirit of the space-obsessed 1960s. A 180 m high, hourglass-shaped tower is topped by a rotating flying saucer that houses a restaurant and observation deck.

ALASKA H O

GERMANY

$ TRADE $

UNIVERSITY CITY, MEXICO

WHEN: 1949–1952
WHERE: MEXICO CITY, MEXICO

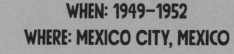

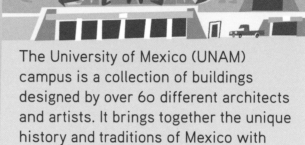

The University of Mexico (UNAM) campus is a collection of buildings designed by over 60 different architects and artists. It brings together the unique history and traditions of Mexico with the ideals of Functionalism.

Functionalism was a mid-century philosophy, which was linked to socialism. Functionalists believed that the look of a building should reflect the function that it served and that it should improve the quality of life of its users.

The campus was built on a bed of volcanic rock. The landscaping of this unusual topography was a key part of the university's plan, providing students with outdoor space in which to socialise.

The design of the university reflects the revolutionary spirit of 1950s Mexico, which aspired to create a fair and equal society rooted in the country's unique history.

PLUS

ULTEA

PTOLOMEO

COPERNICO

UNAM's buildings have Modernist, stripped back structures, but they are decorated with elaborate murals. The Central Library has mosaic murals on each of its four sides depicting Aztec mythologies and scenes from Mexico's colonial past.

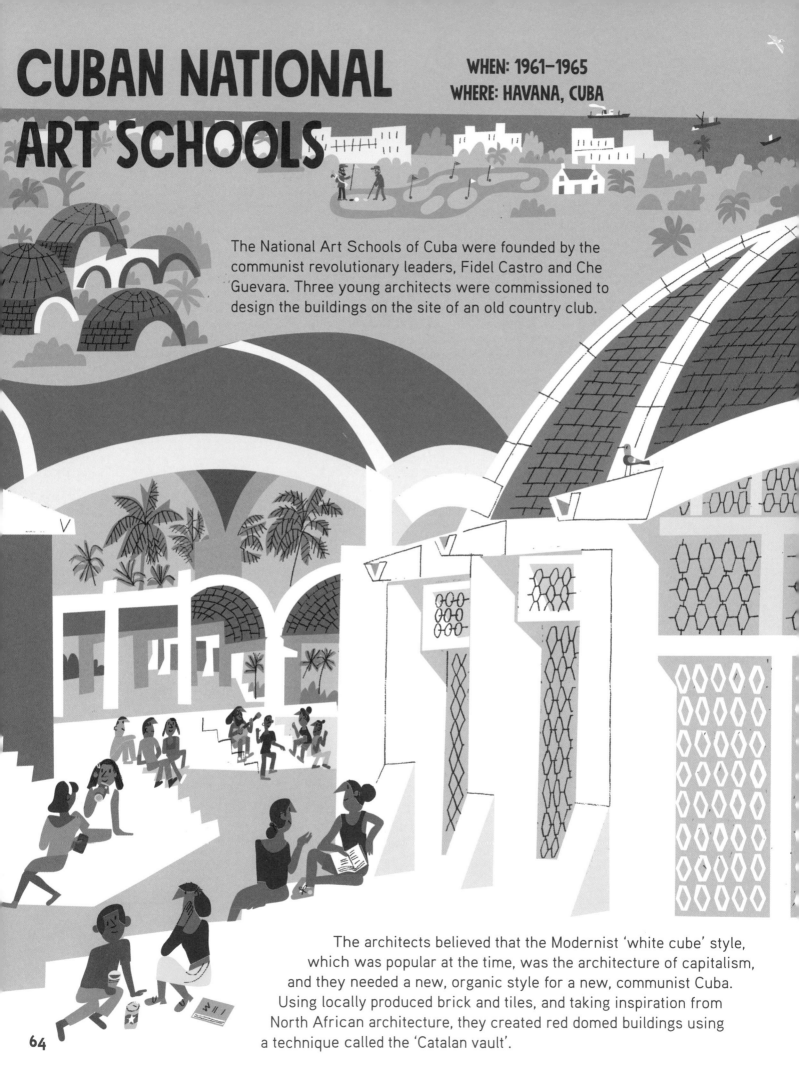

CUBAN NATIONAL ART SCHOOLS

WHEN: 1961–1965
WHERE: HAVANA, CUBA

The National Art Schools of Cuba were founded by the communist revolutionary leaders, Fidel Castro and Che Guevara. Three young architects were commissioned to design the buildings on the site of an old country club.

The architects believed that the Modernist 'white cube' style, which was popular at the time, was the architecture of capitalism, and they needed a new, organic style for a new, communist Cuba. Using locally produced brick and tiles, and taking inspiration from North African architecture, they created red domed buildings using a technique called the 'Catalan vault'.

At first, Castro was very much in favour of the design. However, as Cuba became more embattled, his interest in the buildings waned, and he began to think of the art schools and their architects as frivolous.

The Brutalist Soviet style of raw concrete architecture became more popular in Cuba and in 1965, the building of the art schools came to a halt. The architects fled the country in disgrace.

The buildings were abandoned, unfinished. They were rediscovered in the 1980s and have now been declared a national monument.

SEA RANCH

The Sea Ranch is a collection of private homes along a 15 km stretch of California coastline. The land was bought in 1963 by architect and planner, Al Boeke, who commissioned a group of architects to design houses that would preserve and reflect the area's natural beauty.

66

The houses are compact in size and built in clusters around shared open spaces. They have big windows to maximise the ocean view and sloping shed-roofs to withstand the strong winds. Built of redwood with no overhanging eaves and no unnecessary lighting, they were designed to feel integrated into the landscape.

One of the most striking buildings is the Sea Ranch Chapel, with its sculptural winged roof. Inside, it is decorated with mosaics. The ceiling is studded with shells and sea urchins.

The Sea Ranch was designed as a 1960s utopia; a community that would live at one with the natural surrounds. It has mostly managed to preserve those ideals and has inspired much environmental architecture today.

FIDAK

WHEN: 1975
WHERE: DAKAR, SENEGAL

The International Trade Fair of Dakar (FIDAK) was built as part of a movement sweeping through Africa, in which a new, post-colonial style of architecture was sought, merging local traditions with the popular Postmodern and Brutalist styles of the era.

As there were no architectural schools in most parts of Africa, European architects were commissioned for these bold new projects. The resulting buildings were very expressive and dramatic, often reflecting the architect's impression of a country rather than its reality.

In the case of FIDAK, two French architects, Jean François Lamoureux and Jean-Louis Marin, designed a sprawling trade venue made up of over 20 concrete buildings with soaring triangular roofs. The buildings are connected with walkways and ramps, creating a pattern of diagonals.

FIDAK, like many other buildings in Africa from this time is not loved by the local population, which sees it as a continuation of colonialism, not a response against it.

Although it is still in use as an event and concert venue, many parts of it have fallen into disrepair.

NEW MODELS FOR LIVING

Architects are always looking for new ways to build affordable but comfortable housing for growing populations. Over the past hundred years, architects have had to respond to various challenges, including how to reconstruct bombed environments, how to squeeze houses into tiny spaces, and how to make the most of new technologies and materials.

Cite Radieuse
Marseille, France, 1947–1952

Le Corbusier was a radical architect who designed a high-rise block that would offer spacious city homes with shops, restaurants and sports facilities, all within the same building. He used raw concrete because it was more economical and 'honest'; an approach that became known as Brutalism.

Habitat 67
Montreal, Canada, 1967

Designed by young architect Moshe Safdie for the 1967 World Expo, this building is made up of 350 identical prefabricated concrete boxes arranged in various combinations and stacked on top of one another, like Lego.

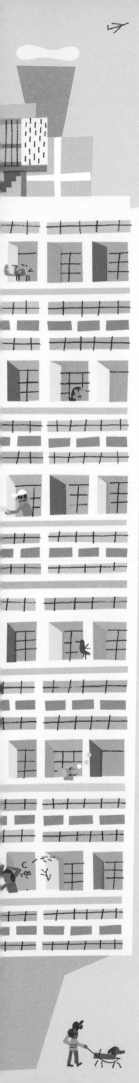

Eames House (Case Study 8)
California, USA, 1949

Husband and wife design duo, Charles and Ray Eames, designed a house and studio made of concrete and prefabricated steel. The grid of the house's frame is broken up with panels in primary colours. Influenced by Japanese architecture, the house sits harmoniously in the landscape.

Paper Log Houses
Kobe, Japan, 1995

After an earthquake devastated the coast of Japan, architect Shigeru Ban sought an efficient solution for the 200,000 people who had lost their homes. He designed houses made of paper tubes with tent material for the roofs. They were cheap, weatherproof and easy to assemble. The materials could be recycled afterwards.

HUNDERTWASSERHAUS

WHEN: 1983–1985
WHERE: VIENNA, AUSTRIA

This apartment building is a striking patchwork of colours, mosaics and organic shapes. There is not a single straight line to be found. Even the floors are crooked!

It was designed by the artist turned architect Friedensreich Hundertwasser, who wished to create a 'House for Human Beings and Trees'.

He worked with architect Josef Krawina to create a building that gave as much back to nature as it took. Over 900 tons of soil were used to create green roofs and terraces. Trees grow through the centre of the building, their branches poking out of windows.

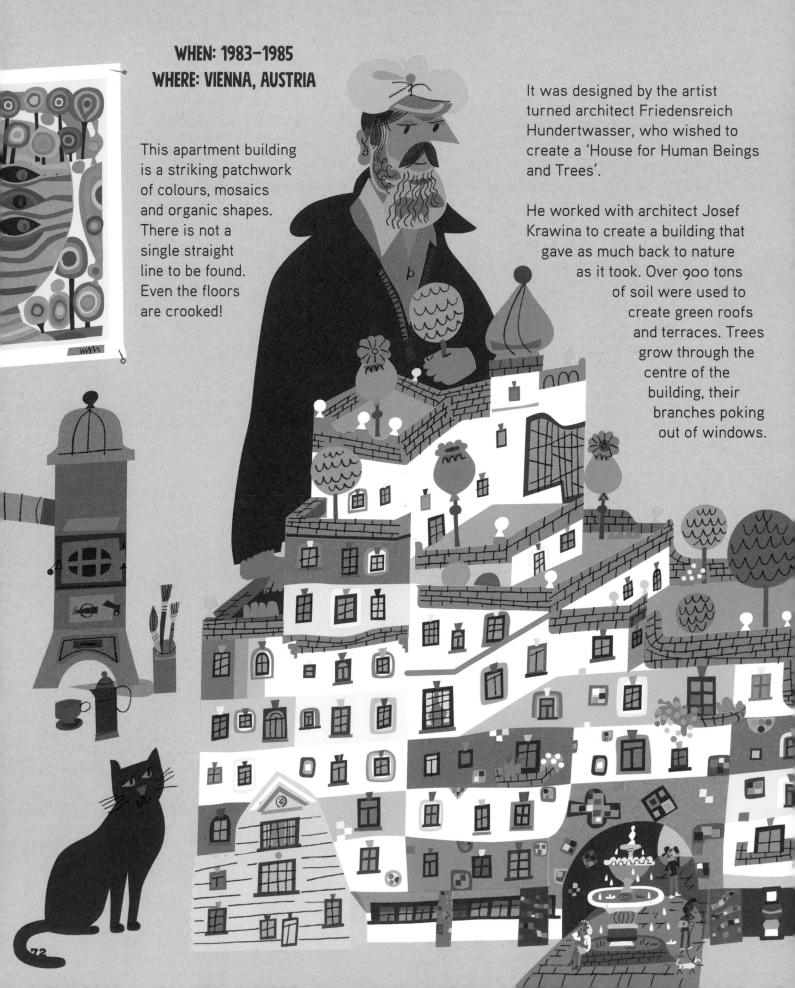

The windows are all different shapes and sizes. Window boxes were considered to be places where residents could express their own relationship to nature.

Hundertwasser believed that columns were an important part of Western architecture: 'Next to a column one feels as under a tree. A column must be beautiful and colourful and shine in the rain and in the moonlight of its own accord.'

The building was mocked when it was completed, but it is now seen as a way for architecture and nature to be in harmony, and is a much loved Vienna landmark.

GUGGENHEIM BILBAO

WHEN: 1991–1997
WHERE: BILBAO, SPAIN

This contemporary art museum sits alongside the Nervion River in Bilbao, Northern Spain. The side of the museum that faces the street is quite a modest limestone and glass building, but when viewed from the river, its true nature is visible. Dramatic, swooping titanium panels resemble the sails of a ship or the scales of a fish, layered on top of each other, catching the sun.

The inside of the museum reflects some of the features of the surrounding landscape. A narrow passageway to the entrance hall looks like a gorge, and a curved walkway echoes the shape of the river.

In the centre of the museum is an atrium that the architect, Frank Gehry, nicknamed 'the flower'. Gehry is an architect known for his expressive, sculptural approach to building design.

The Guggenheim transformed Bilbao from a poor industrial city into a major tourist destination drawing 20 million visitors a year. The 'Bilbao effect' is a term now used to describe the power of star architecture to change the fortunes of a city.

JEWISH MUSEUM BERLIN

The first Jewish Museum
in Berlin was founded in 1933
to showcase Jewish history and
creativity. It was shut down by the Nazis
in 1938. 50 years later, a competition for a
new building was held and it was won by a young
architect called Daniel Liebeskind.

WHEN: 1992–1999
WHERE: BERLIN, GERMANY

Liebeskind designed a new building
next to the old building in a radical zigzag
shape. The only connection between the two
buildings is an underground passage.

The Garden of Exile is a
square of concrete columns, topped by
weeping willows, arranged on a sloping
surface. Walking between them creates a
sense of disorientation and claustrophobia.

A series of empty spaces about 2o m tall cut through the building. These voids represent the sorrow at the heart of German-Jewish history.

The Holocaust Tower is a tall, narrow, empty room with no heating or air conditioning. The only light comes in from a small slit in the roof.

The building is considered Deconstructivist, because it deconstructs and fragments traditional architectural shapes. This fragmentation makes us feel unsettled, so that visitors are not just seeing the contents of the museum but experiencing it emotionally.

NEW MODELS FOR WORSHIP

For almost 2,000 years, the church was an institution more powerful than any other, determining how people lived and how they worshipped. In the second half of the 20th century, more individual ideas of faith emerged, and the architecture of Christianity began to find new shapes.

THE HOLY BIBLE

GOD IS

LOVE

LO

I'M A SINNER PLEASE COME UPON MY HEART

Salvation Mountain
California, USA, 1989-2011

A large-scale artwork made from adobe bricks, tyres, windows, car parts and paint that covers a hill with quotes from the Bible and Christian sayings. It was made by eccentric visionary, Leonard Knight, who spent 30 years living in the back of his truck while he constructed this personal expression of his faith.

Brasilia Cathedral
Brasilia, Brazil, 1958-1970

A sculptural cathedral designed by Oscar Niemeyer. 16 curved concrete pillars take the shape of a crown, open to heaven. They are connected by huge fibreglass panels, flooding the space with natural light.

Hallgrimskirkja Church
Reykjavik, Iceland, 1940

Rising high above the city, this Expressionist church resembles the mountains and glaciers of the surrounding landscape, relating worship to nature.

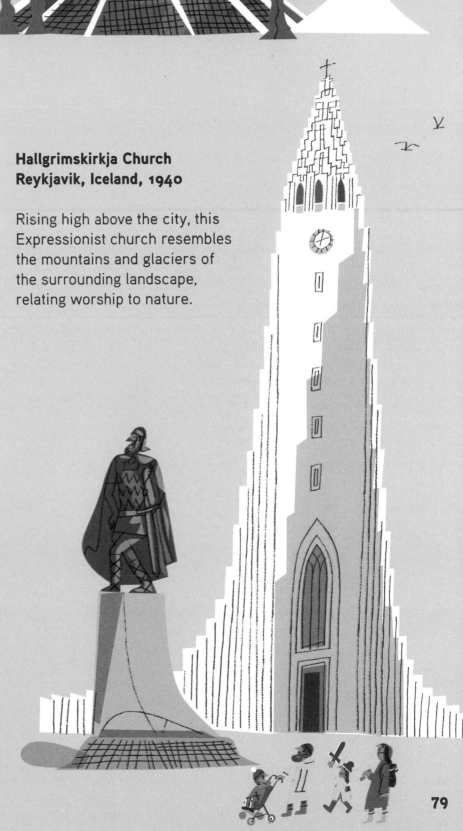

Maria, Königin des Friedens
Neviges, Germany, 1968

A Brutalist church made of raw concrete, with a jagged, crystal-shaped roof. Inside, the main space is dark, whilst the altar is lit dramatically through stained glass windows.

AIRPORT ARCHITECTURE

International travel became much more commonplace in the late 1950s. New airports were built that captured the glamour and excitement of a connected global future.

Control Tower, O'Hare International Chicago, 1970

The air traffic control tower at O'Hare airport was the first of many designed by Chinese-American architect, I M Pei. It has a slim shaft that flares out into the control centre at the top, reflecting Pei's interest in natural forms.

Terminal 3, Shenzhen Bao'an China, 2010-2013

This modern airport in the fast-growing city of Shenzhen is designed in the shape of a manta ray; a fish that seems to fly. Shiny surfaces make the travel experience feel smooth and effortless.

**TWA Flight Centre
New York City, 1959-1962**

This futuristic terminal was designed
by architect Eero Saarinen. It has a
wing-shaped roof that looks like
it might take flight itself.

**Tegel
Berlin, Germany, 1974**

This hexagonal Brutalist
airport reflects the youth and
idealism of its architects. It is
optimised for efficient travel,
but doesn't take into account
security and retail, which are
so important today. It is no
longer in use.

81

SGAE HEADQUARTERS

WHEN: 2008

WHERE: SANTIAGO DI COMPOSTELA, SPAIN

These headquarters for SGAE (the Society of Authors and Publishers) is a building of two sides. One side is translucent glass, facing the street. The other side, which faces a park, is made of huge slabs of stone stacked on top of and leaning against one another in a seemingly haphazard way. This side of the building looks a bit like a Neolithic monument.

The architects, Ensamble Studio, placed the stones at dynamic angles, so that the building seems as though it has collapsed in on itself; like an ancient ruin, whose original structure remains a mystery.

The building is very sculptural, and viewed from the park, feels integrated into the landscape.

Inside, a wall made of CDs reflects the broken light that comes through the jagged stone wall. At either end of the long, narrow building are two big windows framing the view.

HIDEAWAYS

In today's world, space can be hard to come by. These buildings make the most of a tiny space, and relate to the natural or urban world around them in an interesting way.

Dragspelhuset
Årjäng, Sweden, 2004

Translating as 'accordion house' this dramatic extension to a 19th century lakeside cabin can be expanded in the summer to form a big, airy space, and retracted in the winter, creating a cosy, double-walled 'cocoon'. It has an organic, lizard-like shape, covered in cedar shingles that merge with the rocks around.

Parasite House
Quito, Ecuador, 2019

This tiny dwelling is perched on a rooftop. Measuring only 12 m², it has all the basic necessities (bathroom, kitchen, bed, living space) in the smallest possible space. It is a prototype that can be produced cheaply to be placed on rooftops all over the world.

**The Truffle
Candamo, Spain, 2010**

This building was constructed from the inside out. A space was carved out of the ground and filled with hay bales. Concrete was then poured between the ground and the hay. The concrete shell has a natural shape and texture, making it look like a giant truffle.

**Final Wooden House
Kumamoto, Japan, 2008**

This hideaway looks like a Jenga game with half the pieces removed. Long, rectangular cuboids jut out into the space so there are no floors or ceilings. People can climb over it like a landscape and use the blocks of wood however they see fit.

GLOSSARY OF ARCHITECTURAL TERMS AND STYLES

Adobe bricks
Bricks made of mud and clay baked in a kiln and coated in lime. This technique has been used since prehistoric times.

Arcade
A series of arches supported by columns.

Arch
A curved or pointed structural element that is supported at its sides.

Art Deco
A style of art, design and architecture of the 1920s and '30s that combined craftsmanship and luxurious materials with the geometries and modern styles made popular by cubism and abstract art.

Bauhaus
An influential German art school that took a new approach to design combining ideas of aesthetics, functionality and mass production.

Brutalism
A style of building that makes a feature of its materials and mode of construction. These buildings have rough, unfinished surfaces, usually of raw concrete. They have a massive-ness that is accentuated by unusual shapes, straight lines and small windows.

Byzantine architecture
A style of building that emerged in Constantinople under the rule of Roman Emperor Justinian between 527 and 565 CE. Byzantine churches featured large domes and elaborate mosaics.

Buttress
A support that projects from a wall to support the weight of an arch, roof or vault.

Cantilever
An unsupported overhang such as a flagpole sticking out of a wall.

Classical architecture
Architecture inspired by the buildings of Ancient Greece and Rome.

Colonnade
A series of columns that support a string of continuous arches.

Column
A supporting pillar consisting of a base, a cylindrical shaft, and a capital on top of the shaft. Columns may be plain or ornamental.

Constructivism
A style of abstract art that originated in Russia in 1915. It was pared back and geometric, reflecting modern, industrial society.

Deconstructivism
An approach that 'deconstructs' a building, playing with its forms and volumes to create asymmetrical, dynamic shapes that give the impression that a building has been fragmented.

Eaves
The edge of a roof that overhangs the exterior wall, protecting it from rain.

Expressionism
An architectural style that emerged after WWI, reflecting both the horrors of war and a utopian view of the future. Architects used new materials such as concrete to create sculptural, emotive buildings, often inspired by natural forms.

Façade
The exterior of a building (usually the front).

Floor Plan
The arrangement of rooms in a building.

Fluting
Shallow, vertical grooves in the shaft of a column.

Frieze
A decorative band of sculptural reliefs.

Functionalism
The idea that the function of a building should inform everything about how it is designed. With close ties to socialism, the members of this movement believed that architecture should create a better world for people.

Gable
The triangular upper part of a wall at the end of a ridged roof.

Gothic architecture
This style evolved from Romanesque architecture in Europe of the 12th to 16th centuries. Tall, slender buildings featured pointed arches and large stained-glass windows. Flying buttresses were often used for support.

Grotto
A small, picturesque, water-filled cave that can occur naturally or be man-made.

Half-timbering
A timber framework in-filled with masonry or plaster.

Joinery
Woodworking joints in carpentry.

Mihrab
A semi-circular niche in the wall of a mosque that indicates the direction of prayer.

Minaret
A feature of Islamic architecture – a tall spire with a round or cone-shaped crown that is used by the imam to call people to prayer.

Modernism An architectural style that was popular before and after WWII, which rejected decorative elements in favour of clean, simple lines using the latest technologies of concrete, glass and steel.

Monolithic architecture
Buildings that are carved from a single piece of material, usually rock.

Nave
The main body of a church where the congregants sit.

Pagoda
A tiered tower with multiple roofs arranged around a central structure. Common in Buddhist temples of China, Japan and Korea.

Post and lintel
A system in which two upright elements (the posts) support a third, horizontal element (the lintel), to create a large open space beneath.

Portico
A covered walkway made of a series of columns and arches in front of a building.

Postmodernism
A movement that rejected the restraint and seriousness of Modernism in favour of a playful approach to colour, decoration and sculptural shapes.

Romanesque architecture
A style popular in medieval Europe of the 6th to 11th centuries, which featured heavy, fortress-like buildings with thick walls, round arches and large towers.

Stone circle
A circle of large standing stones from the late Neolithic period, usually found in Northern Europe and Britain. It is thought they were used for religious purposes, but nobody knows for certain.

Veranda
A roofed porch that often wraps around two or more sides of a building.

Vernacular architecture
Traditional, local methods of construction using local materials – usually for small buildings like houses.

Ziggurat
A stepped pyramid temple of ancient Mesopotamia.

INDEX

For Hélène, Joyce, Elis, Minou and Batman.

Thank you to Mum, Dad and Paul.

Thank you to Ziggy for building this book and
Frédéric Venditti for building Villa Marguerite.

-PA

Atlas of Amazing Architecture

Text © Peter Allen and Ziggy Hanaor
Illustration © Peter Allen

British Library Cataloguing-in-Publication
Data.

A CIP record for this book is available
from the British Library
ISBN: 978-1-908714-87-9
First published in 2021

Printed in Poland

Cicada Books Ltd
48 Burghley Road
London NW5 1UE
www.cicadabooks.co.uk